SMOKY MOUNTAIN ELK
Return of the Native

MW00679029

SMOKY MOUNTAIN

ELK

Return of the Native

BY ROSE HOUK

**Great Smoky Mountains
Association**

©2013 Great Smoky Mountains Association

Written by Rose Houk
Edited by Steve Kemp and Kent Cave
Design and Production by Lisa Horstman
Editorial Assistance by Julie Brown and Cynthia Slaughter
Front and back cover photographs by Bill Lea

2 3 4 5 6 7 8 9

ISBN 978-0-937207-73-4
Printed in Canada

Great Smoky Mountains Association is a nonprofit organization which supports the educational, scientific, and historical programs of Great Smoky Mountains National Park. Our publications are an educational service intended to enhance the public's understanding and enjoyment of the national park. If you would like to know more about our publications, memberships, and projects, please contact:

Great Smoky Mountains Association
P.O. Box 130
Gatlinburg, TN 37738
865.436.7318
www.SmokiesInformation.org

SUSIE NEEL

CONTENTS

INTRODUCTION   8

AN EASTERN BEAST   12

WHAT IS AN ELK?   19

HOMECOMING   35

FROM EXPERIMENT
TO PERMANENCE   53

AN ELK YEAR   63

ACKNOWLEDGMENTS   71

SELECTED READINGS
& SOURCES   72

INTRODUCTION

Joe Yarkovich sat in the cab of his truck, tapped his pencil on a clipboard, and shook his head. He was looking hard at three lines he'd drawn on a topo map, but those lines weren't telling him what he wanted to know. The lines triangulated radio signals he had just picked up around Black Camp Gap on the Blue Ridge Parkway, hard against the North Carolina border of the Great Smokies.

Catawba rhododendron and flame azalea spangled the roadside on the early June day. Yarkovich had been cruising the road most of the morning, stopping several times, putting on a headset, and sweeping the air with an antenna, listening for the beeping signal from Cow #15. He hoped to zero in on this particular cow because he suspected she had just given birth, or was about to. Number 15 was already well known; she was a matriarch of the founding herd of elk in the Smokies and showed a remarkable ability to learn where to give birth to assure her calves survived.

Facing page: a bull elk sniffs a new calf, but it's anyone's guess if it's his offspring

A newborn elk calf remains on the ground for about a week before being able to stand and run.

THIS PAGE: JOE YARKOVICH; FACING PAGE: BILL LEA

But these rumpled mountains are tough terrain to locate a cow in, much less a small, motionless calf hidden in an impenetrable tangle of shrubs, high grass, and trees. Yarkovich knew he might be getting false signals here, and that's what he surmised had led him on this wild goose chase.

Just the day before, he had found a calf nearby and was able to slide a radio collar around its neck to track it. That calf was the offspring of cow #99 that had moved up out of Cataloochee Valley onto Balsam Mountain to have her young in safety and seclusion. But when Joe came back the next day and searched, he couldn't relocate her or her offspring.

His goal, during this prime calving time for elk, was to collar every calf within days of birth. But finding every calf is a long and laborious task, looking for the proverbial needle in a haystack in a maddeningly random search. And on his clipboard was a list of at least twenty more cows that might be

A cow elk adorned with ear tags and radio collar. Bringing elk back into the Smoky Mountains was a long process, and a closely watched experiment in wildlife management.

BOTH IMAGES: MICHAEL COLLIER

pregnant and ready to drop their calves. Yet even if Yarkovich and his coworkers didn't find and collar every single calf, ultimately for him "the biggest thing…is their survival."

Yarkovich is the lead biologist on the project to reintroduce elk back into Great Smoky Mountains National Park. He succeeds Kim DeLozier, long-time park wildlife biologist who retired from his job in 2010. DeLozier garners a huge portion of the credit for getting the project going and sticking with it through thick and thin.

Underlying the decision to return elk is the National Park Service's founding legislation—its "organic act"—which includes the mandate to conserve parks for "the wildlife therein." And Park Service policy supports reintroduction of native animals when feasible. Among native mammals that once lived in the Great Smokies, bison, fishers, and mountain lions are officially gone, and an attempt to bring back red wolves failed in the 1990s. The other big native mammal, the eastern elk, had been absent for nearly 200 years. But elk reintroductions had been successful elsewhere, and there was strong support from the Rocky Mountain Elk Foundation to try them in the Smokies. Still, these days any attempt to usher an animal back into its wild home is not as simple as just turning a few loose and watching what happens.

Managers in the Great Smokies had plenty of fundamental questions to answer before releasing this big herbivore back into this environment: would the elk find suitable habitat, what would they eat, would they reproduce, would they be healthy or bring diseases, what would prey on them, would they stay put or would they wander?

"People didn't really know what elk were going to do," Kim DeLozier allowed. But as a national park, he saw it as "our responsibility to ask what we could do. So we took a chance." As the project developed, at least as much time was spent on logistics, financing, monitoring, politics, and legalities as on the basic biological concerns. "Everybody was watching what we were doing," DeLozier added. "We were under a microscope."

Though elk are native to the East, and eminently adaptable animals, it was never a given that they would thrive in the Southeast. The effort was purposefully called an experiment to start, one that turned out to last more than a decade. But the elk have survived, and the herd has slowly increased in numbers. It appears, with the return of the elk, the already intricate symphony of life in the Great Smoky Mountains now has a new strain.

Many questions surrounded the plan to bring elk into the park. This cow and bull right beside the Balsam Mountain Road appear to be adapting to their new environment.

An Eastern Beast

Bull elk lock antlers in a sparring match near the Oconaluftee Mountain Farm Museum. This behavior has been shaped over long evolutionary time.

When people think of elk these days, they typically think of big-antlered majestic animals roaming free in the big parks and high mountains of the western United States. Mention elk in the Smoky Mountains and most people immediately ask "were there elk in the East?" There definitely were, but they have been gone for a very long time.

Maps show the range of the eastern elk subspecies nearly solid from the Mississippi River across the Midwest and the Southeast, most everywhere but northern New England and the seaboard. They were in the Appalachian Mountains, and the Great Smokies sat close to the far southern edge of that former range.

Elk teeth and bone and elk pictographs drawn on rocks have been found in the Midwest, but archaeologists have not unearthed any artifacts in the Smokies region. Native people were known to have hunted elk for meat, hides, bone, and antlers, which were used to work stone. The teeth—especially the two upper canines known as ivories, whistlers, or buglers—were especially valued, mostly for decoration on clothing. The Cherokee, who were living in the southern mountains long before white settlers arrived, most likely hunted elk too.

Written, historical records of elk date back to the earliest days of European entry into the Southeast. John Brickell, in a natural history of North Carolina published in 1737, declared "The Elk is a monstrous, large, strong and swift Beast…plentifully to be met with in the Savannas near the Mountains, and Heads of Rivers." But the large swift beasts survived in that state only until about 1750. Naturalist William Bartram noted them in the early 1770s, observing "there are but few elks, and those only in the Appalachian mountains."

In Tennessee, a trader traveling to the Cherokee towns in the late 1600s reported an immense store of game including elk, and others observed them into the late 1700s. Even in the early 1800s, S.N. Rhoads said, "this noble animal was probably a visitant to every county in the state, abounding in the high passes and coves of the southern Alleghenies, frequenting the licks near the present site of Nashville, and roaming through the glades and canebrakes of the Mississippi bottoms."

But by the mid 1800s, elk were largely gone from the southern Appalachians. They vanished early from North Carolina, and the last one in Tennessee reportedly was shot in 1865. Along with overhunting, eastern elk were brought to extinction by private land ownership and destruction of their habitat. So by the late nineteenth century, they were gone forever from that formerly extensive range.

In the entire country, the elk population was astounding—one estimate has ten *million* of them from coast to coast and from Canada down into Mexico when the first Euro-Americans arrived. But along with bison, elk numbers would drastically decline, so seriously that a huge public outcry ensued

Hunters prepare to ship elk carcasses at the train depot just outside the north entrance to Yellowstone National Park in 1906. Similar unregulated hunting practices were a major contributor to the extinction of elk in the East by the 1800s.

by the late nineteenth century. This wanton destruction was a main motivator in establishing Yellowstone National Park in 1872; Yellowstone became a refuge for elk and the central source of those animals in repopulating much of the country. Rocky Mountain elk were transported all over the continent, including several eastern states in the early twentieth century. But poaching and disease led to failure of most of those reintroductions, and by 1922 only about 90,000 elk remained in the nation.

With modern game laws, changes in land management, and acquisitions of large parcels of land, things improved. Though millions of acres of potential habitat have been identified in the East, there is no connecting corridor elk might follow from west to east. So, reintroduction by human effort has been the only alternative for their recovery. And in some eastern states, herds have prospered. In Kentucky, especially, the transplanted elk herd has grown to upwards of 10,000 animals, taking advantage of reclaimed strip mines. Tennessee, Arkansas, Pennsylvania, Michigan, and Wisconsin have managed successful reintroductions too, and other states are looking at the possibilities again.

But Great Smoky Mountains is the first national park in the East to undertake this ambitious project. And with eastern elk absent for so long, biologists knew they had a lot to learn about this creature.

Two bulls and a cow graze on a reclaimed surface mine in Kentucky, an eastern state that has seen striking success reintroducing elk.

BOTH IMAGES: JEFF LAUTENBERGER

Cow elk peer through fencing from an enclosure in Missouri. The penned elk are fed and watered daily, but access to them is limited. A similar pen was used for the soft release in the Smokies.

Elk are large mammals comfortable in meadows like this one in Cataloochee.

WHAT IS AN ELK?

MICHAEL COLLIER

Wild turkeys gobbled bugs out in the meadow, and dragonflies darted from sunflower to sunflower on a serene, peaceful morning in Cataloochee Valley over on the North Carolina side of the Smokies. Large silhouetted figures emerged out of the veil of mist that hung over the meadow. They were cow elk, a half dozen or so, in sleek palomino coats bent to their leisurely morning grazing. They raised their heads and perked their ears when they heard a coyote howl from the surrounding hills.

The cows stayed out in the grass-filled pasture for only a couple hours after dawn, disappeared into the forest during the day, then came back out again before sunset. Their movements almost exactly tracked the line of mountain shadows across the valley. Elk won't be out when the sun is fully up because their bodies cannot take heat. These are animals that adapted to the cold of the far north, where they first arrived in North America. In these southern mountains they have adjusted their behavior to accommodate that physiological fact.

Elk evolved at least thirty-five million years ago, their ancestors a small, semitropical, deerlike animal.

Cow elk graze in the meadows in Cataloochee, site of the park's reintroduction. Cool, early mornings are good times to see elk.

Numbered eartags were attached to every elk initially brought into the park.

KAREN LAWSON MOBLEY

But, writes author Michael Furtman, "By the time of the Pleistocene, elk were elk." That is, at the time of the last ice age they had taken shape as the large, long-legged herbivore we know today as elk.

During the Pleistocene, around 100,000 years ago, a thousand-mile-wide bridge of land spanned the Bering Sea. Elk found their way across this bridge from the Old World into the New, homesteading in Alaska and Canada where they adapted to the glacial climate. As the ice melted and the land bridge was drowned, the North American elk was separated from its ancestors, the red deer, that still live in the Old World.

Once in North America, elk continued to move south and east into the mountains and plains and across the Mississippi River—wherever they found good forage, water, cover, and room to roam, elk did well. They dispersed into many different habitats, from high cold climes, to grasslands, to eastern hardwood forests. Different climates, predators, and seasonal foods gave rise to regional variations or true biological subspecies, depending on who you ask. Yet the basic outline of the animal called "elk" remains—hoofed vegetarians with an even number of toes; with antlers; and with a four-chambered ruminant stomach.

Elk belong to the cervid family, kin to moose, caribou, and deer. The great taxonomist Carolus Linnaeus named them *Cervus elaphus* from the red deer he knew in his home country of Sweden. They are the second largest member of the group—only moose are bigger. In the Smokies, though, elk are now the largest mammal. No question, these *are* big animals. A seven- to ten-year-old male elk weighs about 700 pounds, in some cases upwards of 1,000 pounds, several hundred pounds more than a large white-tailed deer. Female elk, or cows, are a little smaller, normally about 500 pounds. Too big to hide, elk are built to flee from predators by running. Their long legs and hooves let them run, trot, canter, or gallop across hard ground, sometimes as fast as a thoroughbred racehorse. The legs, muscular haunches, and straight back form an elegant animal that awes most people who cast eyes upon them.

To support such size, elk are eating machines—a single animal may take in twelve to twenty-four pounds of forage a day. As with any plant eater, teeth are immensely important. Elk push food back onto their molars and grind it up with lots of saliva, readying it to enter the ruminant stomach. The multi-part stomach was a useful adaptation that let them eat both grass and browse (twigs, leaves, branches). It enabled them to rework these coarser foods in each stomach compartment to render them more digestible. After eating, an elk sits down while the food goes into the first chamber, the rumen, where it is mixed and fermented by microbes. Some of the food is regurgitated, rechewed and swallowed again; then it passes in succession through the reticulum, omasum, and abomasum where it is further fermented before entering the intestine, to be absorbed as nutrition for the animal.

DON MCGOWAN

A bull wears a headdress of vegetation, adornment that probably makes him more noticeable to prospective mates.

An outward feature of these handsome creatures is their coat, one that must inspire envy in their cousins, the white-tailed deer. Elk fur is sleek and tawny, and their necks are shawled in dark brown manes. The distinctive cream-colored rump patch gave rise to the common name *wapiti*, a Shawnee word that translates as "white rump." The lighter summer pelage changes to darker gray in winter, when they add a wool-like undercoat. When they shed from winter to summer coats and back again, they look a bit like they just rolled out of bed.

But the part of elk anatomy that really draws attention is the impressive headgear. Antlers, which alone have been the topic of entire books, are not horns; they are living bone that grows from small knobs on the head called pedicles. Antlers appear on bull elk (females can have antlers but that's a rare aberration) and are grown and shed each year, governed by testosterone levels. At a year old, a male sports his first antlers, usually just small "spikes." Each spring thereafter antlers appear again, adding an inch or so in size every couple of days over three or four months. During a bull's prime, his antlers increase in size and complexity every year. A healthy, mature male, say about seven or eight years old, might sport a "rack" with at least a dozen tines, weighing sixty pounds and spanning more than four feet. Grass alone will not supply the necessary calcium and phosphates for healthy antlers—his diet must also include browse.

FACING PAGE: KAREN LAWSON MOBLEY; THIS PAGE: BILL LEA

Facing page: elk spend a good bit of their time eating, to nourish their large muscular bodies.

Left: a handsome bull elk displays an impressive multipronged set of antlers

In summer, antlers are covered with blood- and oil-rich tissue called velvet. Bulls rub the velvet off on trees just before the fall rut, or breeding season, leaving a tell-tale scent that announces their presence and supposed power. By late summer all the velvet is finally removed, and the antlers are hard and polished in readiness for the rut. By late winter or early spring the antlers drop, and new regrowth begins almost immediately.

Antlers have everything to do with elk reproduction. The bull with the biggest, showiest rack—like a candelabrum alit on his head—is best poised to ward off competitors during the rut. Even more, that crowning headgear advertises to females that he would by far make the best dad. From late September through October—the season of the rut—the bulls wallow in the mud, spray urine, bugle, and generally make their presence unmistakably known, all in an attempt to gather up the largest harem of cows.

And though bulls appear to be masters of the herd, mating will occur only when the females are ready. Cows are in estrus for a short period of time—about twenty-four hours—and only two or three times during the season. Once bred, a cow's pregnancy lasts eight and half months, a long gestation typical of large mammals, humans included. When the birth is imminent, she separates from the herd and goes into seclusion in May or June of the following year, well timed for the greenest food and favorable weather. Also as with most large mammals, she will bear only one calf and will closely tend it during the earliest days. The spotted newborn stays well hidden and immobile for the first week or two of life, but is

Above: bull elk shed their antlers every year and grow new ones.

Right: bull elk rub their antlers on trees to remove the velvet and mark their territory.

A big bull like this one spends a tremendous amount of energy during the rutting season.

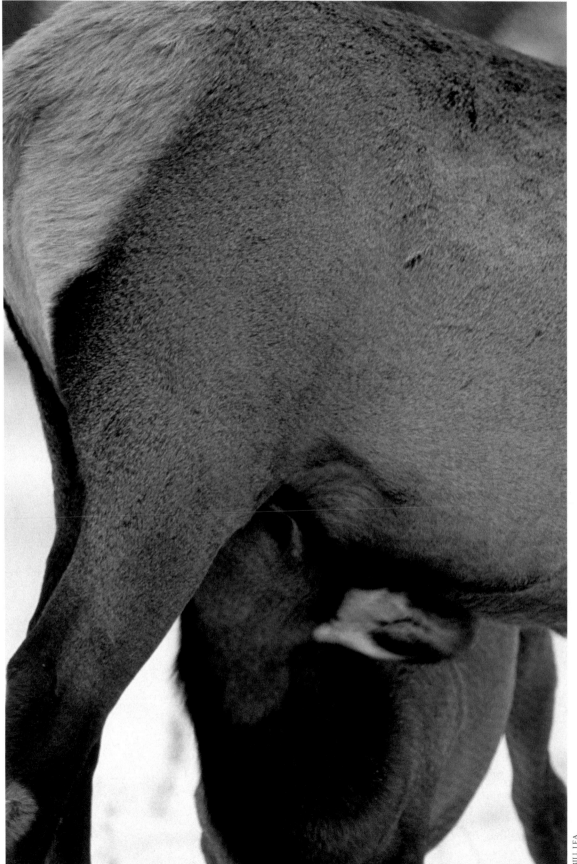

BILL LEA

BILL LEA

This page: a calf nurses at every opportunity, grows quickly, and will soon be on its own.

Facing page: Cow #95 of the Smokies herd, always on close watch.

soon up running and jumping, staying close by mom to nurse on her solid-rich milk. Weighing thirty-five to forty pounds at birth, a calf will gain a phenomenal 150 pounds before it's six months old, filling out on mother's milk but also on plants it will soon find on its own.

Most of the time elk look fairly calm and unconcerned, spending several hours of a day either munching grass or leaves, or laying down beneath the trees. But not to be fooled, they have incredibly fine-honed senses that are always tuned in. Their widely spaced Hepburn eyes afford an expansive field of view, the better to detect shapes and slightest movements of potential predators. A deep preorbital gland at the corner of each eye, like a tear duct, produces scent-filled secretions and flares when an elk is frightened or angry. They have keen hearing, and raise their ears, tip them forward, or rotate each ear independently, to pick up sound. Taste and smell help them choose foods and communicate with one another. If you watch elk for any length of time, you'll note they're often making exaggerated movements of their lips and tongues to "taste" their environment. In this way, they detect all kinds of odors and chemical signals from urine, feces, skin glands, and breath, sharing an olfactory language that can

reveal a male in rut, a female in estrus, or a calf nearby and safe.

Elk communicate in other ways too, sometimes not so subtly. Their legs crack and click as they move through thick cover, perhaps a signal to other elk that friend not foe goes there. A bull may hiss, raise its front legs, or even charge in the face of threat or surprise. A cow elk will aggressively defend her calf by chasing an intruder. Elk will also avert their eyes and turn away to indicate a desire for harmony with another of its kind.

Perhaps the ultimate adaptation is the herd lifestyle that allowed elk to become partial grazers out in the open with some measure of safety. The security of the herd means pregnant cows and calves are better protected, and means all the animals can spend their time and energy getting the best foods rather than constantly worrying about predators. Elk authority Valerius Geist calls it the "selfish herd"—safety in numbers but with each individual still looking out for itself. A herd lessens the chance of any one animal being caught by a predator, and it leaves fewer animals in vulnerable positions. Thus only the slower, weaker animals on the outer edges of the herd are most likely to fall prey. The herd also defines elk society, assuring that each animal honors the hierarchy—the matriarch cow and the superior bull—to avoid competition and conflict.

Though the herd provides security, elk are still prone to particular parasites and disease. Meningeal worm, or brain worm, is known only in the East and lives harmlessly in white-tailed deer. But the parasite can kill elk. Its life cycle is complex and circular, starting with larvae that live in land snails. During feeding, an elk may consume the snails, the worm then moves from the animal's stomach into the brain, causing loss of coordination and paralysis. The cycle continues as the parasite's eggs pass through the elk's digestive system, into feces, then back to snails. Deaths from meningeal worm may have doomed some earlier elk reintroductions in the East.

Bovine tuberculosis is a disease reported in elk, bison, and moose from Elk Island National Park in the 1950s. It waned after the population was reduced, but was diagnosed later in free-ranging elk from Manitoba. The herd brought into the Smokies was certified TB free, and the disease has not been detected in the Southeast yet. It is not contagious to humans.

Brucellosis is a bacterial infection in elk, bison, and cattle, and was present in elk in the greater Yellowstone area by 1930. Aborted fetuses result, and the infection is transmitted by contact and ingestion of infected fetuses. It is most prevalent in the West, especially if animals are overcrowded on wintering grounds. Brucellosis was found and eradicated in the cattle herd in Cades Cove in the Smokies in 1972, and records show the park free of the disease since then.

Of greatest concern these days is chronic wasting disease (CWD). It is contagious among cervids, hard to diagnose, and fatal to elk and deer. Technically a transmissible spongiform encephalopathy, CWD is similar to "mad cow" disease (though it's not known to spread to humans) and to scrapie in sheep and goats. The possible cause is an infectious protein called a prion that accumulates in an animal's brain and leads to central nervous system disease

KAREN LAWSON MOBLEY

Facing page: a bull spends part of its year in solitude, away from the herd.

and death. An infected elk will lose weight, drink more water and urinate more often, grind teeth, salivate excessively, and have head tremors. Advanced signs are severe emaciation, drooling and disorientation, and loss of bodily functions, but aspiration pneumonia may kill the animal even sooner. CWD is thought to be transferred orally from animal to animal or from the environment to an animal. Elk can be watched for symptoms, but no test exists to detect it when they're still alive. Definitive diagnosis comes only by brain or nervous system examination during a necropsy. Chronic wasting disease was first detected in Colorado in 1967, spread to captive and wild elk and deer as far east as Wisconsin and Illinois, and has been found in elk and deer in nineteen states and two Canadian provinces. Biologists and veterinarians were keenly aware of these diseases and the need to take every precaution to assure no infected animals were reintroduced in the Smokies.

Even with healthy elk, other factors have to be taken into account. Elk sometimes are called a "keystone" species, playing several roles in any ecosystem in which they live. As large herbivores, what they select to eat will influence the vegetation of an area. They can affect other ungulates, notably white-tailed deer in the case of the Smokies. Once shed, their antlers become important sources of calcium for small mammals. Elk are also a significant prey species to those predators that manage to take them down. To complete the circle, their carcasses become a source of food for other animals and scavengers.

While recognizing these key roles, biologists rank elk among the most manageable species. Much is known about what they require and what their responses will be. To the public who enjoy observing them, they're something of a "flagship" species. But to farmers and landowners, elk are known to do some damage to gardens, crops, and property.

Even with the benefit of all this general knowledge, people knew repatriating this animal called "elk" in the Great Smoky Mountains would pose challenges.

BILL LEA

Above: elk do have predators, in this case a coyote feeds on a carcass. Coyotes will take calves, but in the Smokies black bears have proven to be the most successful predators. For a time, bears had to be live trapped and relocated away from Cataloochee Valley during the calving season to allow the herd to grow.

Facing page: a cow crosses the road in Cataloochee, trying to avoid a vehicle.

Hundreds of people came on the day in February 2001 when elk were first released into the national park.

HOMECOMING

The idea of reintroducing elk in the Smokies circulated as early as the 1930s, when the first park superintendent, Ross Eakin, received suggestions to bring them back. In reply to a letter from The Camp Fire Club of America, Eakin wrote, "there can be no doubt that the park was formerly a habitat for elk and ordinarily we would consider reintroducing them." But citing poor results of an earlier reintroduction in nearby Pisgah National Forest, he concluded "it is not thought at this time that elk will be reintroduced in Great Smoky Mountains National Park."

Fifty years later the idea resurfaced. In the late 1980s, Kim DeLozier was approached by local members of the Rocky Mountain Elk Foundation, then a new national conservation and hunting organization. "We [the park] had already done peregrines, otters, and started with the red wolf," DeLozier noted, and all but the red wolf had proved successful. Maybe, he thought, it was time for elk.

As it turned out, Kim and his cohorts would follow a long, winding road to get them here. A seemingly endless series of meetings, discussion, and debate ensued. Neighboring farmers came out in force, expressing worries about possible damage to their gardens and cornfields if elk strayed out of the park. DeLozier, an east Tennessee farmer himself, acknowledged the risk, passed out his phone number, and urged them to make their concerns known.

Other issues loomed large, especially disease and parasites that might hurt the elk or be transmitted to livestock—among them the well-known meningeal worm, bovine brucellosis and tuberculosis, and the worrisome chronic wasting disease.

Suitable habitat in the park was a question too. Would these large herbivores find enough grass and browse to eat, or would they end up outstrip-ping vegetation or negatively affecting rare plants? Would they take to the high grassy balds, the Appalachian Trail, or Cades Cove? What about the park's numerous black bears, along with coyotes and bobcats, which could prey on elk calves? Would illegal hunting be a problem?

In 1996, University of Tennessee graduate student Bob Long completed a feasibility study. After evaluating habitat in the park, he concluded that the park's 520,000 acres were more than adequate in size for elk, though open grazing lands were at a premium (only about three percent of the park's total acreage). Bulls and cows would have ample space for home ranges, there was critical cover to hide newborn calves, and the animals would find plenty of water and browse. Admittedly, many of those conclusions were based on limited experience in the handful of eastern states that had reintroduced elk. As Long pointed out, "elk in the East are totally different critters" from those out West, which had received much more study. The only way to test the idea was to bring in elk and see what they would do.

In 1998, then-park superintendent Karen Wade wrote to Elk Island National Park in Alberta, stating the park's "likely need" for fifty elk from their surplus

BOTH IMAGES BY SUSIE NEEL

Park wildlife biologist Kim DeLozier spearheaded the elk reintroduction.

Below: before release, a radio collar was attached to every elk to track each animal's movements and activities.

herd. These were "Manitoban" elk, believed to be the closest genetically to the vanished eastern elk. Perhaps more important—certainly to veterinarian and agricultural interests in North Carolina—the potential transplants had to be closely inspected and declared disease-free.

The release plans received a lot of press through the late 1990s, but it was stop-and-go for a while before all the pieces of the puzzle started to fit together. A key piece—funding—came from outside. Most of the money, just shy of a million dollars, was raised by the Rocky Mountain Elk Foundation, with additional contributions from Friends of the Smokies and the Great Smoky Mountains Association.

In the summer of 2000 the park issued a draft

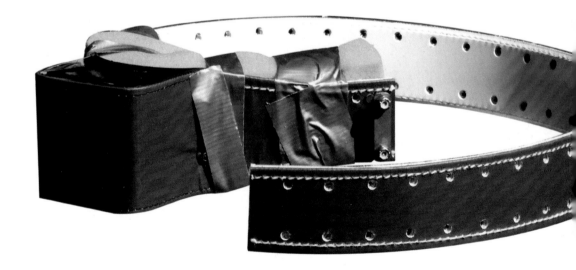

This page, above: elk were trailered into the acclimation pen from Cataloochee Road.

Right: much public interest and the work of many volunteers made the release possible.

Facing page: elk cows emerge from the travel trailer into the acclimation pen where they spent several months before being released into the wilds of Cataloochee.

environmental assessment for public comment. The favored proposal was for an "experimental" release of elk into the remote valley of Cataloochee on the North Carolina side of the park that would last five years. (Four other locations in the park were evaluated—Bone Valley/Hazel Creek, Cades Cove, Parson Branch Road, and Mount Collins on the crest of the mountains along the Appalachian Trail). That October the procedural path, at least, was finally cleared. Yet with eastern elk long extinct, a founding herd would have to be moved over long distances, judiciously released, and monitored far into the future.

The task of transporting the elk and making them comfortable in their new home was aided by many volunteers, among them Ray and Ramona Bryson. The couple first got started by attending banquets of their local Rocky Mountain Elk Foundation chapter, but had no idea they would ever see elk in western North Carolina. Until they met Kim DeLozier. Then it began to look like a possibility.

Ray, a plumber by trade, and Ramona, a retired school teacher, pitched in with gusto. "It's been a life story for us," Ramona declared. The couple lent their hands building the holding pens for the new arrivals, while others donated lumber, fencing, and gating materials and trucked it all in to Cataloochee over the narrow, winding road. Ray devised a line to deliver drinking water to the pens. The elk would be held in the three-acre enclosure on the old Harrison-Caldwell farm and fed hay for eight to ten weeks while they acclimated to their new surroundings. The pens were part of a designed "soft" release, easing the animals in gently and gradually rather than turning them loose immediately in a "hard" release.

It was December 2000, Ramona recalled, when "all of a sudden Kim called and said 'we're going to get some elk!'" They would pick up the first twenty-five animals at Land Between the Lakes on the Tennessee-Kentucky border, a refuge that held the Manitoban elk that had originated at Canada's Elk Island National Park. Ray and Ramona signed on for the trip, and the following month they arrived at Land Between the Lakes. The elk—thirteen bulls and twelve cows and calves—were tranquilized, captured, and blindfolded. To avoid conflicts or injuries the bulls' antlers were removed, and the cows and calves were put into separate trailers from the bulls. It was a nonstop drive back to Cataloochee, arriving in the wee hours of the morning.

To great fanfare, on February 2, 2001, nearly 600 eager onlookers gathered to witness the historic moment. When the trailer doors were opened that Friday morning, four bemused elk clattered through a chute and into the acclimation pen—the first elk to set foot in the Great Smoky Mountains in nearly two centuries.

The following Monday, Kim DeLozier emailed Ray and Ramona, thanking them for their "willingness to support me and this project from beginning to end." His pleasure in the arrival of the elk was great, but even more was "meeting new friends and working toward a common goal." His last words in the message: "Be thankful—Elk are back in NC." Of course, Ramona pasted a copy of that treasured email into one of her bulging scrapbooks that documented the whole process.

After two months, on April 2 the gates of the pen were opened in the presence of another large crowd. As writer Hal Herring described, the day dawned

Cow #5, a member of the first group of elk brought into the Smokies.

Elk are both grazers and browsers, and they find plentiful food to eat in the Great Smoky Mountains.

MICHAEL COLLIER

Above: the prospect of seeing elk has brought crowds of people and their vehicles to once-peaceful Cataloochee. The park has had to respond to a doubling of visitation to the remote area.

Facing page: elk have become accustomed to people, and they tend to cross roads without much concern. Unfortunately, several elk have been struck and killed on U.S. 441 in recent years.

very cold, but the morning sun burned off the frost on the fields. A trail of hay was laid out of the pen to entice the elk, but to the dismay of photographers and observers, they took their sweet time coming out. By afternoon the animals were still trying to make up their minds. Who knew what was in the minds of the elk? The whole affair had to have been a tad disorienting—being captured, blindfolded, and loaded in trailers; driven hundreds of miles; sequestered, fed, and watered by humans; bombarded by a new swirl of sights, sounds, and smells. But by day's end, all twenty-five animals had moved cautiously as a group out of the pen and down the hill into the open pastures of Cataloochee Valley—to a kind of freedom that was beyond their experience. During those first few days, Kim DeLozier urged everyone to give the elk plenty of room. "They are still strangers in a strange land," he said, "and will need space and time to adapt."

Eight of the cows in that group were pregnant, and in June one of them gave birth to a strapping forty-pound male calf, in a blackberry thicket near the release site. It was another red-letter day for the new elk herd in the Great Smoky Mountains. (That calf grew into a healthy bull that lived for at least seven years. But after his radio collar fell off, park biologists lost track of him and his fate is unknown.)

As planned, a second group of twenty-seven animals was brought in the following winter. Those came directly from Elk Island in northern Alberta. Again, Kim DeLozier, the Brysons, and others made an epic journey—2,200 miles in four days, nearly fifty hours each way, and in bitter cold. A third planned release of another twenty-five elk did not happen when the state of North Carolina banned imports of

BILL LEA

A tranquilized elk is fitted with a new radio collar by wildlife biologists as volunteers assist.

elk and deer because of concerns about the serious chronic wasting disease.

Still, what mattered most to Ray Bryson was this: "We've proved that elk can live in western North Carolina."

Once the elk actually arrived and began to settle in, they became the source of many "teachable moments," more than anyone might have imagined. Every elk was ear-tagged and radio-collared for tracking, involving a delicate process of tranquilizing the animals. Drug cartridges are loaded into a dart gun, usually a modified .22, and the shot is delivered from about fifty yards away. The tranquilizer dosage will put an elk out for about an hour. The drugs were chosen for the distinct advantage of being reversible; but sedation of elk carries the risk of aspiration and respiratory problems and an intolerable rise in the animal's body temperature. If their temperature approaches 105 degrees Fahrenheit, they are in distress. To humans handling the drug, even a small amount is a potent toxin if it comes into contact with mucous membranes. Once anesthetized, the animal is blindfolded to lessen the trauma while biologists do a "workup"—taking measurements and hair and blood samples to confirm health status—all as deftly and quickly as possible.

The radio collar/telemetry system made it possible to know the whereabouts of almost every elk in the herd. And it wasn't long before some elk ventured beyond Cataloochee. Elk #22 was a traveler from the get-go. It roamed some fifty miles into

Clockwise from bottom left: Joe Yarkovich checks the radio collar on a blindfolded cow; Kim DeLozier holds the sedated cow down; Yarkovich completes the workup and readies an injection to reverse the effects of the tranquilizer. The cow is let go as soon as the workup is done.

Tennessee, back to Cataloochee for the rut, then back to Tennessee. Another visited the Jonathan Creek/Suttontown area; a third took up with some cows in Maggie Valley, North Carolina. All three wanderers were ushered back into the park.

Other elk dispersed to Oconaluftee and the neighboring Cherokee Indian Reservation. One day—with artificial turf just installed on the football field at the new Cherokee high school—a group of elk saw an opportunity. Here was a green table set just for them, no invitation required, and naturally they helped themselves. Their presence created quite a stir, phone calls were made, and the elk were quickly removed from the grounds. One elk was a regular at the Harrah's Casino in Cherokee; another tried to steal a quilt off an elderly woman's front porch, but Kim DeLozier was able to assuage the woman and retrieve the interloper.

Dan McCoy was chair of the tribal council of the Eastern Band of the Cherokee when the reintroduction started, and he went to bat for tribal funding for the project. Elk were once a staple food for his people, the skins were used for shelter, and the antlers for ceremony, he explained, and to him it was "an opportunity to bring them back to life." The Cherokee know elk as "the big deer," in their language *Oo Tanah-Ah Wi.*

McCoy said he loves seeing the elk around Birdtown and other places on the reservation. His brother has planted food plots to attract wildlife, including elk. And McCoy has taught his son to hunt with a bow, in hopes there will eventually be a huntable elk population for what he believes is healthier, wild meat to eat.

JOYCE COOPER

From left, Kim Delozier and Joyce Cooper present a plaque from the Rocky Mountain Elk Foundation to Dan McCoy and Chief Michell Hicks of the Eastern Band of Cherokee Indians in appreciation of the tribe's support of the project.

KIM DELOZIER

Kim DeLozier is a big man who has an easy way with people. He's congenial and conversational, and puts you at ease right away. During his thirty-year career in Great Smoky Mountains National Park, Kim handled a lot of big animals—black bear, river otters, elk, you name it. But beyond his skillfulness with megafauna, Kim is known as a real "people" person. He is the first to say that the story of the elk reintroduction is as much about people as about a large herbivore.

His background suited him perfectly to the elk program. He worked a lot with livestock on the small farm where he grew up near the Smokies. Fresh with his degree from the University of Tennessee in Knoxville, Kim went straight to the national park and got a job. That first summer, he camped out on Gregory Bald and hunted feral hogs. He moved on to backcountry patrol, then up the ladder to supervisory wildlife biologist in the park. But no matter his position, he always took the time to patiently answer questions and educate visitors.

During his final decade with the Park Service, Kim spent nearly every waking hour on the effort to return elk. It was never a 9-to-5 job, because wildlife don't operate on the same schedules people do. One day, he had tranquilized a 650-pound bull elk, #7 of the Cataloochee herd. He was trying to replace the bull's radio collar, the first one having been lost in a tangle with another male. But the whole process had taken a little longer than he planned. Darkness was setting in by the time Kim administered the reversal drug. It turned into a bit of a wrestling match as he held onto the animal until the very last minute, to make sure it was fully awake before turning it loose.

This incident spoke volumes about Kim DeLozier's approach to wildlife management. His goal always was to do no harm to the animal. His only higher aim was never to see a park visitor or any personnel hurt in an encounter with an animal. If that ever happened on his watch, Kim considered it a true failure.

One of his worst days during the elk reintroduction, he said, was when he got a call from a furious neighboring landowner. An elk cow and her calf had come onto the man's property and were scaring his cattle. He was so angry he threatened to sue, call the sheriff, and kill the elk. After Kim talked with him for some time, the man relented and even apologized. Kim went over the next day, darted the animals, and took them back to the park.

Kim DeLozier's hands-on work and field knowledge, along with his approachability and openness to other views, earned him the respect of his coworkers and peers. Beyond park circles, nearly everyone he met in the Rocky Mountain Elk Foundation could not praise him enough. Upon his retirement, Kim received a commendation in the Congressional Record—and a nice pair of binoculars.

SUSIE NEEL

MICHAEL COLLIER

The popularity of the elk doubled visitation to Cataloochee. Each year, some 150,000 people drive in for the thrill of seeing, and hearing, the elk, especially during the rut. But the intimate valley wasn't made for such a throng and not everyone is so thrilled. Before the Great Smokies became a national park, a large and prosperous farming community had grown up in Cataloochee Valley; many descendants of those residents still return to visit and reunite with relatives. For locals who fondly treasure this quiet, remote corner of the park, the elk-inspired influx has become something of a sore point. It was expressed by one man—in bib overalls and carrying a lawn chair on his back—as he hiked down the Pretty Hollow Trail with his son and grandson. His mother had been born and raised in Cataloochee, he said, and he wished the elk had never been brought here. He feared the road would be paved out to the interstate, bringing in so many people "you could stir 'em with a stick." His concerns were not without basis. On most afternoons in October, cars and trucks from a dozen states park on the shoulder of the road, cross the one-lane bridge up by the Beech Grove School, and make the tight turnaround at the end of the narrow drive. And the elk, meanwhile, have become quite accustomed to the humans. A few curious animals will come right up and stare into the rearview mirror of a vehicle.

Most visitors are thoroughly captivated by the animals' beauty and behavior. Yet a few have failed to fully grasp that these are wild animals—that a 700-pound bull, or a cow with her calf, could hurt a person if they charged. People are required to stay 150 feet away from any elk, but some shutterbugs can't resist getting just a little closer for the best picture of a bugling bull or a two-week-old calf hopping up out of the high grass. A food handout to any animal is a major infraction. Even the family dog can do real damage. Cow #97 was a sad example. She was run to ground by a pack of hunting dogs and suffered muscle breakdown and weight loss. Though she lived, she was never able to breed or regain full health.

Though they may seem tame, elk are wild animals capable of inflicting serious injuries, especially during the rut and in calving season.

A bull elk drinks from Cataloochee Creek.

THE BUGLE CORPS

The increase in visitation to Cataloochee has brought new restroom facilities, more frequent trash pickup and road grading, and more ranger presence. But a group of volunteers called the Elk Bugle Corps has had the most interaction with visitors on a daily basis. The corps, which began in the park in 2007, performs interpretation and crowd control in the valley. Most of the volunteers are nearby residents who receive training, wear identifiable clothing, and tootle up and down the road in a small electric vehicle. They pull out show-and-tell items like elk antlers, hooves, and hide for visitors to touch. One man drives 150 miles roundtrip to his post; two sisters come in together to work; a retired couple from Florida helps out.

The Bugle Corps volunteers are usually out along the road each afternoon, keeping an eye on people and elk and sharing their own observations. Their payment comes in unforgettable experiences among the elk. As one volunteer described, he was out on a July day when a big storm blew in while the elk were out in the valley. "You can watch the rain off their backs, the little ones start dancing, they're so happy for the coolness," he said. It's the privilege of being part of those special moments that keeps the Bugle Corps volunteers coming back year after year, giving freely of their time.

"Elk guy" Joe Yarkovich explains some biology to volunteers with the Elk Bugle Corps.

A "spike" (young bull elk) runs through the meadow.

MICHAEL COLLIER

FROM EXPERIMENT TO PERMANENCE

The acclimation pen where elk got their first taste of life in the Great Smoky Mountains is still there. It wasn't hard to find, located right beside the Big Fork Trail about a quarter mile in. Ten years later, the ten-foot-high fencing still stood, wrapped in slightly tattered black mesh material. Outside the fence, a raised wooden observation platform was moldering away. Within the fence a healthy growth of small shrubs and vines crowded the ground. Whether the pen would ever be used again was anyone's guess, but it stood as a tangible reminder of the grand experiment of returning elk here.

The University of Tennessee in Knoxville, guided by the U.S. Geological Survey's biological arm and in partnership with the national park, oversaw the research during the experimental phase. Research ecologist Joe Clark and his students have performed most of the investigations. It was one of Clark's students who spent the most time with the founding herd during the earliest days of the reintroduction. As part of her doctoral work, Jennifer Murrow fed and watered the elk in the pen, then followed them without cease after they were released. She collected plentiful and important data during that critical time, and completed her dissertation under advisor Clark.

For Joe Clark himself, most of his experience had been with big mammals, but when he became involved with the Smokies reintroduction, "elk were kind of new species for me," he said. Though the large herbivores had been gone for a long time, some scientists hypothesized that elk might have been partly responsible for keeping the high grassy balds open in the past. That and other reasons sparked Clark's interest. To his mind, the big questions at the beginning were "how well can the elk do in the park and how well can the park do with elk?"

Clark thought Cataloochee was a good choice for the release site because habitat was suitable, there were not a lot of deer, and there was one-way access for better management. Also, he felt the acclimation pen and soft release accomplished what they'd hoped. They were able to hold the animals for a time, do health checks, prevent deaths upon release, and encourage the elk to stick around.

Students and elk researchers conduct a workup during the experimental phase of the reintroduction.

A biology student gets hands-on experience with elk in the Smokies.

His focus was on population dynamics—herd size, birth and death rates, and age and sex composition. Midway through the experiment, signs were hopeful—the herd had topped fifty animals and the elk were reproducing. But on the downside, too many calves were dying. The herd was teetering on the edge, and any slight change meant the chances of extinction were "fairly high," Clark noted. Part of the problem was the smaller number of animals released than originally planned—the third group was never brought in because of North Carolina's ban on imports. The bigger problem was that nearly half the calves were not surviving, and about three-fourths of all the deaths were from black bears. At Land Between the Lakes, the elk had no experience with bears. In Clark's words, "these elk were naïve to any kind of predator…and bears were having a field day."

Enter another of Clark's graduate students, Joe Yarkovich. Raised and educated in Pennsylvania, Yarkovich had worked with lots of different wildlife in other places before taking over the all-consuming job of elk technician in the Smokies. He arrived as the park's elk herd had plateaued at just under 100 animals. People knew elk calves are most vulnerable in the first week of life when they can't stand or run away. The possible solution—keep more calves alive by removing bears during calving time from mid May through June. The thinking was that if new calves could get a jump start on life, if they could

Elk bulls get most people's attention, but biologists look at calf survival as a more important sign of the long-term health of the herd.

KAREN LAWSON MOBLEY

buy some time without bears around to eat them, the herd might start to increase. Thus the bear relocation effort became the topic of Yarkovich's thesis.

From 2006 to 2008, bears were captured in Cataloochee in culvert traps baited with bacon, sardines, and doughnuts. (Biologists learned that bears have a sweet tooth, especially for Krispy Kreme doughnuts. They found a bakery that furnished seconds of that favorite brand, saving some money on bait for the traps.) Tagged and radio-collared, the bears were then driven some forty miles away and released in the Twentymile area of the park. Everybody appreciated that bears, with their strong homing abilities, would find their way back to Cataloochee, probably within a month. But by then the calves would be up and able to escape. During the three-year effort, forty-nine bears were translocated, thirty were tracked, and nearly half of those thirty did in fact return. In the same period, coincidentally, forty-nine calves were born and survival increased. Though this was encouraging, relocating bears was considered a short-term solution, so the effort stopped.

Probably more important to calf survival was that pregnant cows learned to seek private, safer places to give birth. Cows like #15. She had a calf in the meadow in Cataloochee, and a bear killed it. The following year, she found her way up to Balsam Mountain and bore a calf that survived. The next year another cow followed her, and so it went. Consequently, calf "recruitment" improved. It also helped that cows became more aggressive in protecting their newborns when bears or coyotes showed interest.

The adult elk did better too, though about four a year have died from both natural and human caus-

Above: Joe Yarkovich (left) and Kim DeLozier (right) were the two park rangers most involved during the early years of the elk reintroduction.

Elk cows have "learned" to give birth to their calves in places that assure better survival.

BOTH PHOTOGRAPHS BY BILL LEA

es. Causes of mortality have included meningeal worm, collisions with vehicles, and fights among elk. The first illegal hunting fatality was Elk #21, a well-known bull of the founding herd. The animal was found dead in a pasture in Cataloochee in November 2009. The poacher, a North Carolina man, pled guilty to the shooting and was sentenced to jail and fined a sizable restitution. Another original dominant bull, #16, was found dead in the Harmon Den area, its head and antlers removed; three people were charged with illegal possession of the antlers. On private property outside the park around Mount Sterling, another three elk were shot dead.

The experimental phase of the elk reintroduction was extended from the original five years to eight. But in 2009 park officials were at a critical juncture. They had to examine all the evidence and decide if the elk were here to stay—or not. After fielding another environmental assessment, the National Park Service made the decision: the elk program was a permanent reintroduction. After his long involvement, Kim DeLozier was especially gratified. The decision, he said, indicated "that our elk restoration efforts in the North Carolina section of the park have been deemed a success."

A great deal was learned during the experiment.

Bull #21, one of the first in the park, was shot illegally in Cataloochee in 2009. The poacher was caught and prosecuted.

First, the majority of elk did stay close to where they were released. Healthy calves were being born, and more important were surviving. Those born in the park tended also to stay close to their natal ground. What the elk might lack in open terrain appeared to be made up for in the high quality of food. Elk are known to be "mixed feeders," eating mostly grass but also browse. In the Smokies, they have added acorns when plentiful in the fall, and munched a few ferns and lichens too. Their home ranges have stayed relatively small—about eight square miles for males, about four square miles for females. Unlike elk in the West that migrate to lower elevations in the winter, the park herd does not need to move so far because southern winters rarely see much snow.

The 2010 environmental assessment presented four alternatives: keep the status quo, do extremely limited management, remove the herd, or manage the elk as a permanent resource under what's known as "adaptive" management. The park chose the adaptive management plan, to extend for fifteen years, until 2025. It gives more flexibility to make changes as more science becomes available and as the dynamics of the elk herd evolve.

A quartet of bulls, antlers in velvet, grazes peacefully within park boundaries. In 2011, the park declared the elk release no longer an experiment, but a permanent reintroduction.

As the plan got underway the herd was estimated at about 140 animals in and outside the park. Around fifteen to twenty calves were being born each season in the park, and calf survival was close to 80 percent. Those figures added up to a consensus that the elk herd had become self sustaining. Still, the herd's population status, health, and impacts will continue to be assessed in the coming years. Under the scheme, monitoring of individual elk will be much more selective. All possible calves will still be collared, as will some cows and a select few bulls. So with succeeding generations, fewer Smokies elk will sport heavy collars and dangly numbered ear tags. Land management actions will depend on herd needs. Decisions to mow the meadows in Cataloochee, for example, will be based on whether calving is to be encouraged or discouraged. Another technique, prescribed burning, will continue to be used to open up grassy areas and encourage understory shrubs.

The plan also provided that various land-managing entities—federal, state, and tribal—would assume responsibility for elk that have taken up residence outside the park, and that has happened. If any animals become a nuisance, they will be dealt with on a case-by-case basis by a range of methods such as fencing or aversive conditioning.

A distinct browse line has become evident on the edge between forest and meadow in Cataloochee, and the park is monitoring the effects of elk feeding on plants. A series of fenced "exclosures" in different kinds of habitats have been built. Botanists will revisit the exclosures every three to five years to compare growth outside the fence (where the elk feed) and inside the fence (where they don't). They will also do vegetation surveys along established elk trails.

Undoubtedly, they will look closely at the work of Liz Hillard, a Western Carolina University master's student. Hillard spent half a year striding over many miles in and around Cataloochee, identifying elk "hotspots." Tracking elk hoof prints, scat, and other sign, she mapped their favored travel routes. She found that elk tend to take the easiest path through the woods—along ridgetops, manways, and fire trails—that often lead to old settlements. Hillard also collected fecal pellets (those round elk droppings) to discover more precisely what the elk were eating, and she charted some 250 antler-rubbed trees.

No one has suggested a maximum number for the elk herd in the park. Even though open land is at a premium, most people think the elk will find plenty of food to eat. If the animals become too numerous, their natural way of regulating their population is to disperse. And black bears, bobcats, and coyotes will continue to prey on the young or the weak and sick. But if the population should show a big increase, or if the elk cause unacceptable damage, the park's plan allows for moving animals, or even culling the herd as a last resort.

Biologists know they still have plenty to learn about the elk, and huge effort and study of this famed herd will persist. But in Great Smoky Mountains National Park, the noble animals called "elk" will roam free, as wild creatures, to grow and prosper as they will, adding a substantial new element to this landscape. In the process, we will surely see in their eyes a reflection of our own values.

The elk herd will continue to be monitored, and the park will adapt management techniques as necessary. But just the sight of these animals, back in their Smokies home, is a thrill.

BILL LEA

The unmistakable sound of a bugling
bull elk fills quiet autumn mornings
in Cataloochee Valley.

BILL LEA

An Elk Year

On a picture-perfect October morning in Cataloochee, the trees on the hillsides are drenched in autumn's palette, and dried meadow grasses are backlit with gold light. Blue jays scold as they awaken, but mostly all is silence. Suddenly a prolonged, high-pitched screech echoes across the valley. The unearthly sound comes from a premier bull elk, tossing back his heavy-antlered head to give a performance worthy of Pavarotti. It is the vocal expression of the annual fall rut, the elk breeding season. He is announcing to other bulls, and his harem of cows, that he's the KING—at least for today.

He issues a few more moderate bugles, but the cows keep grazing and appear unmoved by his come hither call. He pursues one, but she runs away from his advances. Unfazed by the rejection, the randy guy continues on up toward the Palmer Chapel to another group to see if any other cows are in the mood, and manages to nudge two of them away, expanding his harem to five.

The shorter days of September had already sparked increased testosterone production in the bull, a hormonal surge that marks the beginning of the rut and rules his every move until the end of October. This master will spar with rival bulls, locking antlers in a kind of faux fighting. But if it's a true battle, it will be a crashing, knock-down-drag-out encounter with a decided winner and loser. A fight carries the risk of real injury to the bull—a broken neck, deep wound, or worse. A young spike and so-called "satellite" bull hover around the edges of the action, but they aren't serious competitors.

The whole purpose of the bull's big antlers, and all the bugling, pawing, rubbing, and thrashing, is to attract the largest number of cows and convince them he is the finest specimen of fatherhood. That large, healthy set of antlers on the older, more mature bulls

This page: a young "spike" bull with small antlers must learn the tricks of the trade from his elders.

Facing page: a bull signals his superiority with big antlers and loud bugling.

BOTH IMAGES BY MICHAEL COLLIER

signals good nutrition and thus superior genes to pass along to offspring. The cow comes to recognize the pitch of the bugles, and she is the one that does the choosing. In her second year she's ready to mate; she will entertain the bull's affections by lying down and letting him lick and nuzzle her, or perhaps she'll take the initiative herself. When the couple copulates—during the brief time she is receptive—he rears up on his hind legs, enters her from the back, and completes the act in a hurry. Outward signs of breeding are not obvious, though if bred the cow will not come into heat again during this rut. The bull, meanwhile, keeps up the search for other further opportunities.

As the breeding season winds down, the bull will gather with others of his kind to take time off until the next breeding season. Having exhausted all his fat and energy stores herding cows and fending off other bulls, he will spend the winter refueling and rebuilding his strength. In the Smokies, that means filling his stomach with acorns and other foods available during the quiet dormant season. Meanwhile, the pregnant cow will retreat with other cows, steadily taking in nourishment for herself and her growing fetus. Winter can be a lean time, and though snow is usually not too deep, she will be looking for anything she can find to eat. Good nutrition is the key to everything in elk life.

By March the following year, the wintering group of bulls starts to break up. They will shed their antlers and start to grow new ones. It's the time of greening up in the Smokies, with lots of fresh grass and browse to eat. All the elk are feeding furiously during this most critical time of the year.

BILL LEA

Above: a bull nuzzles a cow, urging her to accept him as her suitor.

Facing page: these bulls may practice by sparring, but no-holds fights do sometimes occur between rival males during the rut.

KAREN LAWSON MOBLEY

Facing page: healthy, growing elk calves are the most encouraging sign that the Smokies herd will do well.

In May or June, after about 250 days of pregnancy, the cow will have a very heavy feeling in her ballooning stomach. With birthing imminent, she goes off alone to find the ideal site with plenty of cover, and food and water nearby where she can have her calf.

This is another busy time for Joe Yarkovich and his coworkers, tracking each cow and looking for newborns. Days start at dawn with a quick tour through Cataloochee Valley to see which cows look like they are seeking seclusion, or it might also involve a trip up to Balsam Mountain or over to Oconaluftee to check on others. Joe suspected Cow #11 was about ready, because she was by herself up a drainage off the Rough Fork Trail in Cataloochee. So on a sultry summer afternoon, he took his telemetry equipment in with a film crew, hiked about a quarter mile up the hillside, and found her there. She warily walked a wide circle around the intruders, who watched from a respectful distance. Joe looked around for signs of calving, but left with the sense that she had not yet given birth.

Then again, a spotted newborn is incredibly well camouflaged and has almost no scent. Right after birth, mom cleans off all the membranes and amniotic fluid from her calf and scours the birth site to remove any scent of the calf. When Joe handles a calf he washes the collar, wears gloves, and does everything possible to keep from imparting any human odor. And though the calf may appear to be abandoned, mom is most certainly close by and watching; should anyone try to come near her calf, she may well charge, as Joe and others have learned all too well. Other than staying close, the cow's main job is to keep eating and producing milk for her hungry young one, milk that will help the calf grow fast and strong and resist disease.

Joe and his assistants repeat the routine daily throughout calving season. Sure enough, a morning check of the meadows found Cow #11, the one Joe had tracked two days before. She had come back down with a wobbly calf in tow and hot on her heels to suckle. She likely had already had her calf when Joe was up in the drainage, then moved back down to the meadow. As summer wears on, other cows and newborns will join in, with some aunties too, forming a nursery herd.

In a good June, a calf can be born almost every day somewhere in the Great Smokies. Joe Yarkovich the scientist may resist showing feelings towards individual elk, but he doesn't apologize for the emotional response he has toward the calves. Without hesitation, he said his most memorable events have been with the calves. "I love finding and catching calves," he said. So small and well hidden, they are hard to find. But "you know it's there, it's a couple days old, you sneak up, grab hold of it…it's all big dark eyes staring up at you…and you realize that's the future of the herd."

BILL LEA

A thriving "family" group—bull, cow, and calf—are proof that elk have at long last made the journey back to the Great Smoky Mountains.

BILL LEA

ACKNOWLEDGMENTS

Joe Yarkovich and Kim DeLozier deserve a hearty thank you for all the time and interest they gave in helping make this book as full and accurate as possible. Their dedication to their work and to these animals is exemplary. Bill Stiver also graciously offered assistance. Ray and Ramona Bryson, Joyce Cooper and Dan McCoy are all deeply involved in the elk reintroduction effort, and do so out of sheer care of the animals. Joe Clark took time to offer his perspectives, and Carolyn Jourdan generously shared some of the many stories she has gathered. Annette Hartigan as always provided all manner of support and encouragement. Steve Kemp has been a stalwart friend and enthusiastic editor through it all. And Michael Collier once again shared in the delight of watching these animals one beautiful fall in the Great Smoky Mountains.

BILL LEA

SELECTED READINGS & SOURCES

Environmental Assessment for the Establishment of Elk (*Cervus elaphus*) in Great Smoky Mountains National Park. National Park Service. 2010.

Furtman, Michael. *Seasons of the Elk*. NorthWord Press, Minocqua, WI. 1997.

Geist, Valerius. *Elk Country*. NorthWord Press, Minocqua, WI. 1991.

Long, James R. Feasibility Assessment for Reintroduction of North American Elk into Great Smoky Mountains National Park. Master's thesis. University of Tennessee Knoxville. 1996.

Murie, O. J. *The Elk of North America*. Stackpole and Wildlife Management Institute, Harrisburg, PA. 1951.

Murrow, Jennifer. An Experimental Release of Elk into Great Smoky Mountains National Park. Dissertation, University of Tennessee Knoxville. 2007.

Petersen, David. *Elkheart*. Johnson Books, Boulder. 1998.

Toweill, Dale E. and J.W. Thomas, eds. *North American Elk: Ecology and Management*. Smithsonian Institution Press. 2002.

Yarkovich, Joseph. Black Bear Relocation as a Method to Reduce Elk Calf Predation Within Great Smoky Mountains National Park. Master's thesis, University of Tennessee Knoxville. 2009.